cELtic
MYTHS AND
LEGENDS

Fiona Macdonald

Raintree is an imprint of Capstone Global Library Limited, a company incorporated in England and Wales having its registered office at 7 Pilgrim Street, London, EC4V 6LB – Registered company number: 6695582

To contact Raintree please phone 0845 6044371, fax + 44 (0) 1865 312263, or email myorders@raintreepublishers.co.uk. Customers from outside the UK please telephone +44 1865 312262.

Edited by Nancy Dickmann and Abby Colich
Designed by Jo Hinton-Malivoire
Original illustrations © Capstone Global Library Ltd 2013
Illustrations by Xöul
Picture research by Elizabeth Alexander
Production by Victoria Fitzgerald
Originated by Capstone Global Library Ltd
Printed and bound in China by China Translation and Printing Services

ISBN 978 1 406 25973 5
17 16 15 14 13
10 9 8 7 6 5 4 3 2 1

Acknowledgements
We would like to thank the following for permission to reproduce photographs: Alamy: pp. 7 (© Skyscan Photolibrary), 15 (© Cro Magnon), 16 (© Ben Molyneux Travel Photography), 18 (© Paul Shawcross), 24 (© Peter Horree), 28 (© The Art Archive), 29 (© The Art Gallery Collection), 31 (© JAM WORLD IMAGES), 35 (© Ancient Art & Architecture Collection Ltd), 38 (© Ancient Art & Architecture Collection Ltd), 40 (© Ancient Art & Architecture Collection Ltd); Corbis: p. 5 (Heritage Images); © English Heritage. Reproduced courtesy of the Trustees of the Clayton Collection: p. 9; Getty Images: pp. 4 (DEA / A. DE GREGORIO), 13 (Werner Forman/Universal Images Group), 14 (Werner Forman/Universal Images Group), 19 (Werner Forman/Universal Images Group), 22 (Universal History Archive), 23 (DEA / G. DAGLI ORTI), 25 (Imagno/Gerhard Trumler); © Laurianne Kieffer - Musée de La Cour d'Or Metz Métropole: p. 12; Rex Features: p. 41 (Moviestore); Science Photo Library: p. 17 (British Museum/MUNOZ-YAGUE); Shutterstock: pp. 8 (© Patryk Kosmider), 34 (© Patryk Kosmider), 39 (© Panaspics); Superstock: p. 30 (DeAgostini).

Design features: Shutterstock (© Vangelis76, © Nancy A Thiele, © Stephen Bonk, © Lukiyanova Natalia / frenta, © Natasha R. Graham, © Lukasz Pajor, © S. Hanusch, © Neil Roy Johnson, © Bobkeenan Photography, © Jiri Vaclavek).

Cover photograph of a panel of the Gundestrup cauldron, 2nd or 1st century BC, reproduced with permission from Corbis (© Heritage Images). Background image reproduced with permission from Shutterstock (© Martin Capek).

The publishers would like to thank Miranda Aldhouse-Green for her invaluable assistance in the production of this book.

Every effort has been made to contact copyright holders of any material reproduced in this book. Any omissions will be rectified in subsequent printings if notice is given to the publisher.

Disclaimer
All the internet addresses (URLs) given in this book were valid at the time of going to press. However, due to the dynamic nature of the internet, some addresses may have changed, or sites may have changed or ceased to exist since publication. While the author and publisher regret any inconvenience this may cause readers, no responsibility for any such changes can be accepted by either the author or the publisher.

CONTENTS

Did you know?

Discover some interesting facts about Celtic myths.

WHO'S WHO?

Find out more about some of the main characters in Celtic myths.

MYTH LINKS

Learn about similar characters or stories from other cultures.

DANGEROUS
NEIGHBOURS?

Proud. Brave. Good-looking. Tall.
Boastful. Quarrelsome – and very
dangerous! That's what ancient Greek
and Roman people said about their
neighbours, the Celts. For hundreds
of years, from around 400 BC to AD
100, Celtic tribes attacked Greek
and Roman lands. So, of course, the
Greeks and Romans feared them.

This bronze statue,
found in Italy, shows
a Celtic warrior god
standing tall, alert and
ready for action.

Although the Celts never wrote their myths down, Celtic works of art, like this huge silver cauldron decorated with pictures of gods and magic creatures, tell us a lot about Celtic people and their ideas.

THE TRUTH ABOUT CELTS

But the Celts were not just fierce fighters. They belonged to a rich and exciting culture. Celtic people loved sport, hunting, feasting, music, fine clothes, and fabulous jewels. They were expert artists, designers, and craft workers. They worshipped awesome gods, and performed human sacrifices to please them. They were also head-hunters – cutting the heads off slaughtered enemies and displaying them on their houses, because heads were highly prized as trophies!

Celtic peoples believed in magic and mysteries, and created myths full of fantasy and adventure. They did not write down these stories, but passed them on by word of mouth. Many have been forgotten, but a few have survived for over 2,000 years. This book tells some of the best-known Celtic myths.

MYTH LINKS

Myths are stories with meanings. They have been told by people from many different civilizations, all round the world. Myths can't be proved like science or maths, but they can tell us truths about good or bad behaviour, relationships, ideas, and feelings. Do you know any modern myths?

A CELTIC WAY OF LIFE

The Celts were powerful in Europe between around 700 BC and AD 400. They were not a race, or a nation. Instead, a Celt was anyone who spoke a Celtic language and lived a Celtic lifestyle.

This map shows where Celtic tribes lived in Europe, around 300 BC.

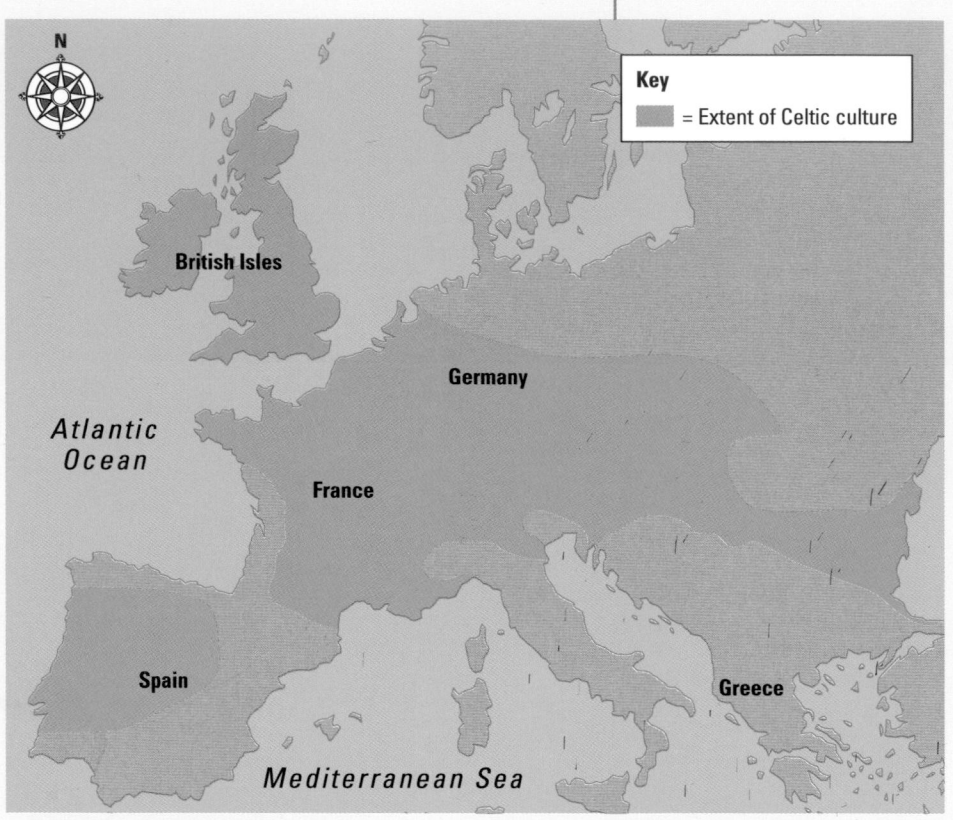

Key

▬ = Extent of Celtic culture

N

British Isles

Germany

Atlantic Ocean

France

Spain

Greece

Mediterranean Sea

Historians think that the Celtic way of life developed slowly, over hundreds of years, as people in Europe created rules for living and fighting, and rituals for worship. They invented new technologies and created new designs. They belonged to many different tribes, but they all used words from the same family of languages.

Tribesmen and women sometimes fought each other, sometimes travelled and traded peacefully, and sometimes married members of different tribes. In all these ways, new words, ideas, skills, and myths spread from one community to another, until people in many parts of Europe shared a similar way of life. The ancient Greeks and Romans called this lifestyle 'Celtic'; we still use the same name today.

Did you know?

In 391 BC, Celtic tribes invaded Italy and headed towards Rome. At that time, Rome was the centre of a powerful empire. In 279 BC, the Celts invaded Greece.

The Celts and the Romans both honoured mythical warriors as leaders of their tribes. The Romans admired wandering hero Aeneas; the Celts praised heroes like the Daghda (*Dah-dah*), a wise, rough, greedy, loving, tribal god who carried a huge war club that could kill and bring back to life.

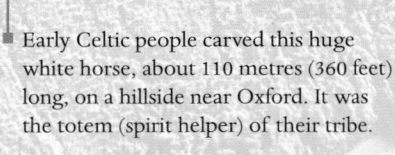

Early Celtic people carved this huge white horse, about 110 metres (360 feet) long, on a hillside near Oxford. It was the totem (spirit helper) of their tribe.

GODS ALL AROUND

The Celtic world was a magical place. The Celts were superstitious and believed that the earth, sky, water, and trees were all alive with supernatural powers. Myths told how, in Ireland, the Stone of Fal cried out when it was touched by the rightful High King.

DIFFERENT GODS

Each region had its own gods and spirits. For example, boar-goddess Arduinna lived in the Ardennes mountains of Belgium. Boann gave her life and energy to the Irish River Boyne. Danu, goddess of the Earth, was worshipped throughout Central Europe and Britain. According to Scottish myths, the blue-faced Cailleach Bheur dropped huge rocks from her apron to make Scotland's mountains, and stirred Scottish seas into a deadly whirlpool whenever she washed her cloak.

Celtic myths also told how gods, spirits, and the ghosts of dead ancestors had homes in another world, close by. Living people could enter this strange, shadowy kingdom at certain special places: rounded, grassy hills, ancient stone tombs, or smooth, shining lake waters.

Many Celtic legends grew up around monuments left by peoples who lived long before Celtic times. This stone tomb was built in Ireland around 3500 BC. The Celts said it was the gateway to the Otherworld.

WHO'S WHO?

Celtic myths from Brittany, France, describe a beautiful nature-spirit called the Groac'h. She lured young men to her home deep beneath lake waters – and kept them there, forever.

MYTH LINKS

Stories from many lands link gods with hills and mountains. In ancient Greek myths, for example, the gods lived at the summit of mighty Mount Olympus.

This stone carving from northern England shows Coventina, guardian goddess of a sacred spring. The Celts believed that its waters had healing powers. When Romans lived in England, they began to worship Coventina.

Balor of the evil eye

Great it was. Grand it was. Long, long ago. When our lovely land of Ireland was home to gods and heroes.

Great and grand it was to live there. But also brutal and bloody. The fights! Ah, the fights! And the warriors! So brave, so fierce, so mighty!

Such terrible, terrible battles! The earth itself shook and trembled. You can still see the scars today. There's one at Loch na Sul; the Lake of the Eye.

And how did it happen? Balor! Balor! A god – and a monster. An evil giant, with an evil eye. A giant eye; a killer. A single glance from it destroyed anything. Anything at all.

Now Balor had a daughter, young and wise and gentle. He kept her in a cave to be all alone, forever. He had been warned that if ever she had a son, that boy would kill him.

But love is clever. Love is brave. Love keeps trying. Young, handsome Kian, a child of the Great Goddess, would not give up. He found the cave and found the girl. They fell in love.

When their babies were born – a magic three, all at once – Balor threw them into the sea. But one boy survived. His name was Lugh. Lugh of the Long Arm, the champion stone-thrower.

Lugh led the armies of the Great Goddess against evil Balor. He stood up. He stepped out. He grabbed a rock and hurled it. So hard it flew. So swift, so sure. So true, so deadly. The power of the Goddess was with him that day, for certain.

Balor fell so fast that his evil eye was still open as his giant head crashed to the ground. Its evil rays burned a huge hole; its tears filled the hole with water.

And so now you know. The Lake of the Eye. That's how it was created!

A LIVING FROM THE LAND

Most Celtic families were farmers; they grew wheat, oats, barley, and beans. They raised sheep, pigs, and cattle, and bred dogs and horses. They worked hard to survive – and asked gods and goddesses to help them.

Strong, swift Epona protected horses and their keepers. Wise, generous Rosmerta, goddess of all growing things, was the "great provider". The Three Mothers sent babies and the Stag-god Cernunnos gave men strength and fertility. The springtime goddess Brigit looked after lambs, while Nantosuelta watched over bees and sent sweet honey.

Nantosuelta was a goddess of fire and fertility. In statues made in ancient Celtic times, she is often shown holding a little model beehive on top of a long pole. To the Celts – and later peoples – bees were symbols of sweetness and productivity.

Many Celtic myths featured farming. Ireland's epic *Cattle Raid of Cooley* told how Queen Medb plotted to steal a magnificent Brown Bull – so big that 50 boys could dance on its back. In other stories, sea-god Manannan owned pigs that were killed and eaten one day and re-born the next. The goddess Brigit had a lake of cows' milk that never ran dry.

■ Strange and powerful, this god, pictured on a Celtic silver cauldron, has antlers like a stag. He is holding a torc (a sign of high rank) and a snake with horns (a symbol of fertility).

Did you know?

Celtic farmers marked the seasons with four festivals:
- Imbolc (*Ih-mollk*) 1 February, start of spring
- Beltene (*Bell-tayne*) 1 May, bonfire-festival, to strengthen the Sun
- Lughnasad (*Loo-nah-sah*) 1 August, harvest-time
- Samhain (*Sow-in* or *Sav-ann*) 1 November, death of the old year

KINGS, QUEENS, AND HEROES

Celtic tribes were ruled by kings, queens, and chieftains. Some real and mythical kings were chosen by magic. In the "Bull-Sleep", a man ate flesh from a bull and wrapped himself in its hide to dream of who should be king. But, more often, kings had to fight to win power. For example, Irish myths tell how King Fergus was challenged by Conchobar, his step-son and rival.

Celtic metalworkers fashioned this statue of a magic bull. It was a symbol of strength, health, and good fortune.

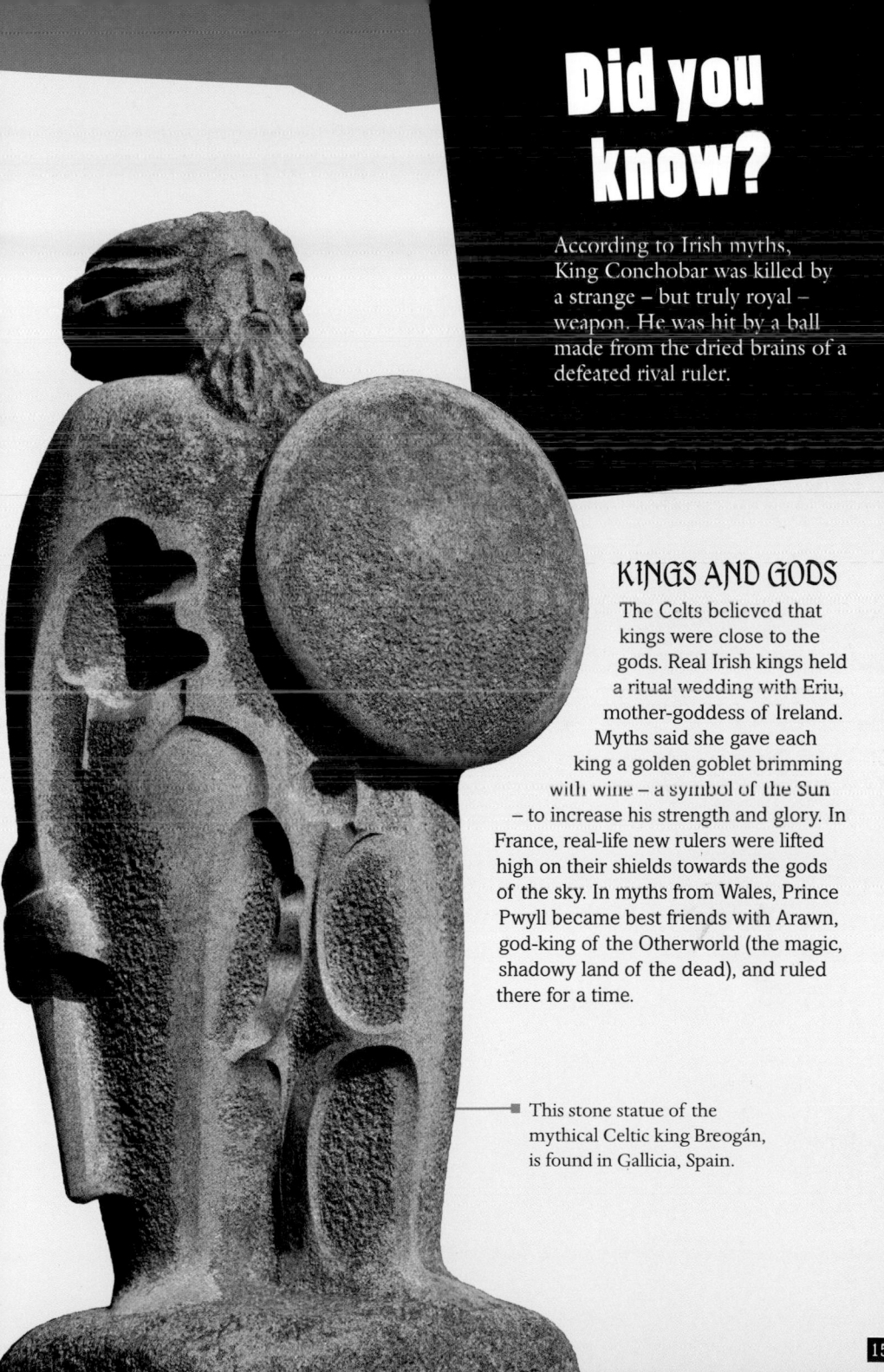

According to Irish myths, King Conchobar was killed by a strange – but truly royal – weapon. He was hit by a ball made from the dried brains of a defeated rival ruler.

KINGS AND GODS

The Celts believed that kings were close to the gods. Real Irish kings held a ritual wedding with Eriu, mother-goddess of Ireland. Myths said she gave each king a golden goblet brimming with wine – a symbol of the Sun – to increase his strength and glory. In France, real-life new rulers were lifted high on their shields towards the gods of the sky. In myths from Wales, Prince Pwyll became best friends with Arawn, god-king of the Otherworld (the magic, shadowy land of the dead), and ruled there for a time.

This stone statue of the mythical Celtic king Breogán, is found in Gallicia, Spain.

THE KING MUST DIE!

Celtic people believed that a king or queen was the living image of their kingdom. If a ruler was strong, honest, and healthy, their lands would prosper. But if he or she was weak or unjust, the kingdom would decay.

Irish myths told how Nuadu had to stop being king after he lost an arm in battle. The god of blacksmiths and magic healing, Dian Cecht, made Nuadu a new arm from silver, so he could rule again. Myths said Dian Cecht could cure anything except a head that had been cut off!

WHO'S WHO?

Queen Boudica ruled the Iceni, a Celtic tribe in eastern England. In AD 60–61, she fought against the Romans. Her warriors destroyed two Roman towns: Colchester and London. But then Roman troops defeated Boudica's army and took over her lands.

This statue shows the strong and powerful Queen Boudica, who led an uprising against Roman forces in AD 60.

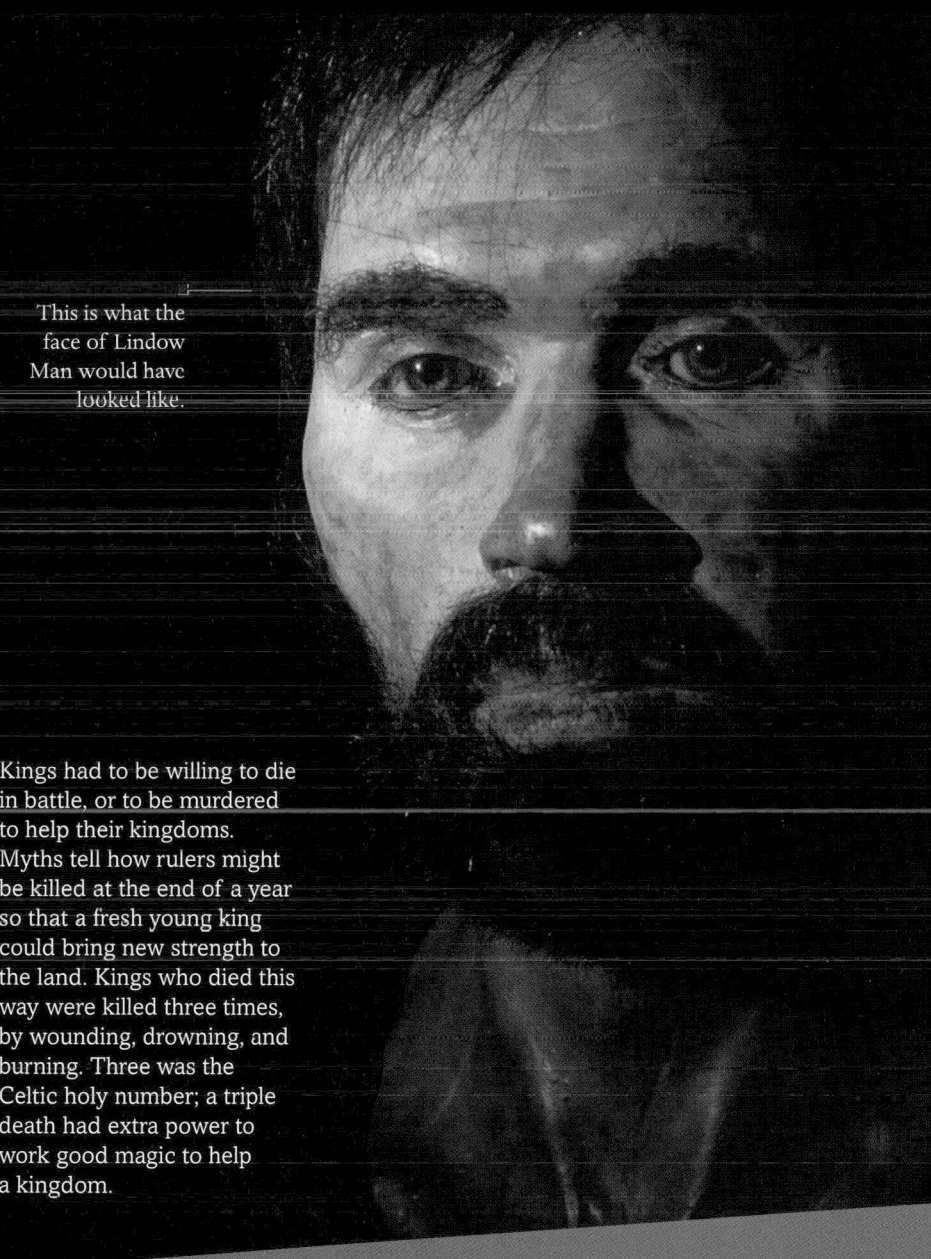

This is what the face of Lindow Man would have looked like.

Kings had to be willing to die in battle, or to be murdered to help their kingdoms. Myths tell how rulers might be killed at the end of a year so that a fresh young king could bring new strength to the land. Kings who died this way were killed three times, by wounding, drowning, and burning. Three was the Celtic holy number; a triple death had extra power to work good magic to help a kingdom.

WHO'S WHO?

The body of "Lindow Man" was found in a bog in north-west England. He may have been a Celtic king, killed around 2,250 years ago to help his tribe. When he died, Lindow Man was young (about 25) and healthy. He wore body paint and a fox-fur arm-ring. He had manicured fingernails and a neatly trimmed moustache.

MAGICAL HEROES

Real-life Celtic kings led armies of brave, loyal soldiers. But in Celtic myths, the greatest fighting men were often part hero, part monster. For example, giant Fionn Mac Cumail was leader of the Fianna, a ruthless band of warriors. He was raised by druids and a witch and could speak with animals.

Stranger still, Irish war-hero CuChulainn had seven fingers and seven toes. His eyes had seven pupils each. His hair was striped in three colours and stood on end in battle. He glowed with a strange, unearthly light, and his bones spun round and round inside his skin. To real-life Celts, mythical characters such as Fionn were great examples of courage and daring, but they would not want to meet them on the battlefield!

AMAZING WEAPONS

Mythical warriors carried supernatural weapons. Fionn had a magic helmet; Conchobar's shield shrieked a warning whenever he was in danger and CuChulainn's three-pronged spear always killed.

In 52 BC, in France, real-life Celtic King Vercingetorix gave himself to the Romans to be executed so that they would not massacre his followers.

This statue of Vercingetorix can be found in France.

Celtic warriors charged into battle roaring and yelling. Their comrades blew carnyxes, giant war trumpets that terrified enemies with their eerie sound.

WHO'S WHO?

The Morrigan was a dangerous, shape-shifting Celtic goddess of love and war. In myths, she hovered over battlefields, protecting favourite warriors. She might appear as one woman or three, or as a magic eel, wolf, cow, or raven.

Did you know?

Kings in France and Switzerland paid for bands of top Celtic warriors to come and fight for them. The warriors fought naked to show that they were ready to die.

A new name

King Conchobar strode across the playing field.

"Who's that?" he asked gruffly. "A new boy? He's young! How old? Only seven?"

"You! New boy!" he bellowed. "Let's test you! Let's see if you're tough enough to start warrior training. Tonight you will guard my horse while I dine with Culann the Blacksmith. Now tell me – what's your name?"

Later that day, Setanta, the new boy, was running as fast as he could. The king had already set off for Culann's house. Setanta must catch up with him!

He was nearly there. But – oh no! – he heard Culann's strong gate closing. The king was safe inside, but what was that, in the darkness? Culann's fierce watchdog, fangs bared, was rushing towards Setanta!

At first, he shook with fear, but then a strange madness seized him. He felt giant-sized, giant-strong. He kicked and bit and stabbed and snarled. He tore, he strangled. Soon, Culann's dog was slumped at his feet … dead.

Culann the Blacksmith spoke first. "My dog! My friend! My beauty!" The king stood grim and silent, while Cathbad the druid, eerie as ever, peered into the future.

Setanta was calm again. "Culann, your dog is dead, but now I will guard you!" he said. Suddenly, the druid chanted out loud: "And you will have a new name: CuChulainn, the Hound of Culann."

King Conchobar sent CuChulainn to live with the other young warriors. Druid Cathbad was their teacher. One morning, he said, "Anyone who takes up weapons today will be a fine warrior…"

Once again, the madness seized CuChulainn. He rushed round the palace, trying out all the weapons he could find. He was so strong that he broke them all, except the king's great sword.

Cathbad found him. "CuChulainn," he said, sadly, "you should have let me finish. Yes, anyone who takes up weapons today will become a great hero. BUT he'll also die young, all alone."

Celtic hunters chased deer and fierce wild boar in the forests. This Celtic statue of a very bristly boar was made in France around AD 100.

RAIDING, HUNTING, BOASTING

When Celtic warriors were not fighting, they went on raids to steal cattle, or practised battle skills. Running, jumping, and wrestling were good training for war. According to myths, sun-god Lugh founded a summer sports festival rather like the Olympics, and hero CuChulainn loved fast, furious games of hurling.

Myths tell us that hunting was Celtic warriors' favourite sport. But hunters respected the animals they killed. They believed that the spirits of dead animals lived on – and might return, to lure hunters into the Otherworld. In myths, Welsh prince Culhwch chased a monster boar wearing jewels in its hair. He was helped by a talking stag – a forest god in disguise.

MYTH LINKS

When the Celtic King Matholwch dipped dead warriors in his magic cauldron, they were re-born. In a similar story, Greek goddess Clotho boiled a murdered baby in her cauldron and brought it back to life again.

FEASTING

When the hunt was over, warriors shared a noisy feast. Minstrels entertained them by singing, playing harp music, and telling stories. The warriors joined in, making jokes and boasting about their adventures.

At feasts, the bravest man was served the "Champion's Portion", the best piece of meat, usually pork. The myth of King Mac Da Tho tells how one feast turned into a riot, as guests fought to be chosen as champion.

This massive krater (cauldron for mixing wine) was buried with a Celtic princess in France around 500 BC, ready for a feast in the Otherworld.

PRIESTS, PROPHETS, AND POETS

Kings and warriors were the highest-ranking people in Celtic lands. After them, druids (Celtic religious leaders) were the most respected. Roman writers said that druids were cruel, evil magicians. But Celtic myths tell us that druids could also be wise and clever.

Scottish and Irish stories tell of druids like Finnegas, who were priests and teachers. They led religious ceremonies and recorded the history of their tribe. They collected useful – and magical – information about plants and animals, or the Sun, Moon, and stars. Their learning was never written down; it took years to memorize.

This life-size metal face mask was made around AD 100. It was found at Celtic holy springs in Bath, England. It might have been worn by a Druid making offerings to the gods.

Celtic myths also tell how druids composed poems praising kings and heroes, or cursing their enemies. After one quarrel, angry Welsh druid Llwyd turned half a kingdom into a desert. Druids also claimed to see into the future.

A tall strong woman – perhaps a priestess – carries a bowl for offerings to the gods in this cult (holy) wagon, buried in a Celtic grave in Austria around 600 BC. Druids and magic stags run beside her.

Did you know?

In a famous myth from Ireland, the druid Cathbad warned that a baby girl, not yet born, would be extremely beautiful – but doomed to a life of sorrow. The baby's name was Deirdre; her love for a handsome prince led to his murder, and Deirdre killed herself rather than marry the evil king who captured her.

The Salmon of Knowledge

Down by the river, Finnegas, the druid, shouted out, "Quick! Look! It's massive – a real monster! Get a move on, Fionn my lad! We can't let it get away!"

Fionn, his pupil, hurried over with the net. By now, Finnegas had hooked the fish, "That's right! Gently does it! Just a flick of the wrist…" Puffing and panting, Finnegas spoke to the fish: "And you, you silver darling, you king among fishes, you hear old Finnegas, too. Always, I've longed to find you. You, the treasure any druid seeks. You, the quick, sleek, shining, splendid, full-of-secrets Salmon of Knowledge."

"Now I've got you. Is it fate? Have the gods arranged our meeting – me the hunter, you the prey?"

"Quick, Fionn! Quick with that net! Look, he leaps…!"

"Phew! We got him! You did well, Fionn. But now I'm exhausted. So you must cook that salmon – but be very careful. I've fixed it on a spit. All you have to do is tend the fire. Don't stare at the fish, or touch it, or eat it!"

Fionn did as he was told. But as he leaned close to the fire, hot fat from the fish splashed on his hand. Quickly, without thinking, he licked the burn to soothe it.

All at once, the world seemed to spin and swirl around him. He could see everything: past, present, future. His brain was suddenly teeming with words, music, numbers, magic, secrets…

Old Finnegas awoke. He peered hungrily at the fish but jumped back, in alarm. "Fionn! Fionn! FIONN!" he bellowed. "What's happened? The salmon's power has gone! Have you disobeyed me?"

Trembling – with excitement at what he now knew, and with fear of his teacher's wrath – Fionn explained what had happened.

Finnegas forgave him. "What's done is done. But all the power of the Salmon of Knowledge has passed into you. Now you're very clever, Fionn – and magic – and dangerous!"

GIFTS FOR THE GODS

The Celts believed that the gods who ruled their world needed to be pleased. So they sacrificed things they valued most, such as food and drink, prize animals, fine weapons, and, occasionally, humans. They threw these things into rivers, lakes, and bogs, burned them, or buried them.

Most sacrifices took place at times of great danger. For example, when Roman armies invaded England, real-life Queen Boudica gave sacrifices (probably wild boars) to Andraste, goddess of victory. In France, ill or injured people sacrificed their pet dogs to river-goddess Sequana, hoping she would cure them.

DEAD ENEMIES

Some of the most precious gifts a Celt could give to gods were heads from dead enemies. To the Celts, the head was the home of each person's spirit. One mythical Irish warrior slept with a dead enemy's head under his knee; he believed it made him stronger. Myths from Wales tell how the head of giant King Bran was carried around by his warriors, cut off but still talking, to bring luck and protect his kingdom.

Celtic treasures like this decorated shield, thrown into a river in London, were deliberately damaged before being given to the gods, to "kill" the spirits that lived in them.

Human skulls stare out from this gateway to a Celtic holy place in southern France. They were placed there as gifts for the gods, and to give the site extra magic power.

MYTH LINKS

Today, 2,000 years after the Celts made sacrifices, people still throw coins into wishing wells, fountains, and pools. Some believe that this brings good luck.

Did you know?

Celtic druids organized sacrifices, and observed them carefully. They believed that the victims' dying movements could foretell the future.

MAGIC AND MONSTERS

In Celtic myths, gods appear as people, humans turn into animals, and women become men. In one story, Oenghus, god of love, seeks a woman he sees in a dream. She transforms herself into a swan, so he does too, to be with her. Together, they lull the whole world asleep by making beautiful, magical music.

The Welsh myth of Blodeuwedd described a girl created from flowers to be a hero's bride. Later, the hero turned into an eagle, while Blodeuwedd became an ugly owl.

A jealous queen changed Irish princess Etain into a rainbow-coloured fly. Welsh stories told of the red-eared Hounds of Annwn. They were messengers from the Otherworld who hunted human souls.

OPENING DOORS

In myths, past, present, and future blended into one. Gods and heroes travelled between life and death. During the festival of Samhain, the doors between this world and the Otherworld flew open, letting ghosts and demons escape.

A Celtic warrior from eastern Europe wore this bronze and iron helmet. The magic raven (a bringer of death) was designed to protect him – and scare his enemies. The wings would flap as he ran along.

The modern holiday of Halloween comes from the Celtic festival of Samhain – a time of ghosts and monsters.

■ Myths told how this ferocious Tarasque monster lived in the River Rhone, in France. It sometimes clambered up on to dry land, grabbing and devouring human prey. It had a wolf's jaws, a lion's mane, and two human heads!

MYTH LINKS

Supernatural dogs feature in the myths of many cultures. For example, the ancient Greeks and Romans told tales of fierce, three-headed Cerberus, who guarded the entrance to the Underworld.

The shining singer

Ceridwen was a goddess – and a witch, so they said. So of course, she had a magic cauldron. It gave singers their notes and poets their words and filled the world with music. The magic took a year to make. It was tricky and dangerous.

One day, the cauldron was full. Morda the Sightless stirred and stirred, while boy servant Gwion helped him. Ceridwen sat on a chair like a throne, watching, watching.

A year is a long time, even in a myth, and Ceridwen felt sleepy. She dozed, and Morda's stirring arm moved slower and slower...

All of a sudden, the cauldron heaved and bubbled. Just three spurting drops of magic fell on Gwion. He suddenly found himself covered with soft brown fur. Then he saw Ceridwen, wide awake and furious, come shrieking towards him. Like the hare he now was, Gwion bounded along, fast, fast, faster. Ceridwen the hound raced after him, hungry jaws slavering.

Gwion leaped into a stream. Now he had fins! He could swim! But snap! Ceridwen the otter's jaws were close behind.

Gwion flapped his fins and soared into the sky. He was a swallow, gliding, swooping. But Ceridwen, a killer hawk, flew towards him.

My only hope, thought Gwion, is to make myself small. He dived into a barn, and became a tiny grain of corn among millions of others.

Ceridwen followed, of course. And now she was a hen. With one quick peck, she gobbled Gwion up.

But witches can't always control their own dangerous magic. Gwion became a baby, growing safely inside Ceridwen. She vowed to kill him as soon as he was born, but he was too beautiful. So instead, she threw him away.

Gwion lived on, still splashed by accidental magic. And he grew up to be the greatest poet in Wales. They called him Taliesin, the shining singer.

THE NEXT WORLD

Celtic myths were full of fighting and dying. But there were also stories about love and joy, peace and plenty – perhaps not in this world, but in the Otherworld, after death. Celtic people believed that the spirits of the dead went on living there. They might rest forever, or be reborn as humans or animals.

Myths told how, for warriors, the Otherworld was a place of feasting and war-games. Otherworld gods like Da Derga kept magic cauldrons that were always full of food, and held brave contests between heroes. For everyone else, the Otherworld was a garden full of fruits and flowers. There was no pain, no sickness, no death. Kindly goddesses like Cliodna lived there. Her magic birds sang sweet songs that eased all suffering.

In myths, the Celtic Otherworld was far, far away in the west, beyond the rays of the setting sun.

However, for anyone who was still alive, the Otherworld could be grim and terrifying. When the brave hero CuChulainn dared to visit, he met staring skulls, twisting snakes (Celtic symbols of death and rebirth), and many bloodthirsty monsters.

Celtic peoples buried their dead will all kinds of valuable objects beside them, ready for use in the Otherworld.

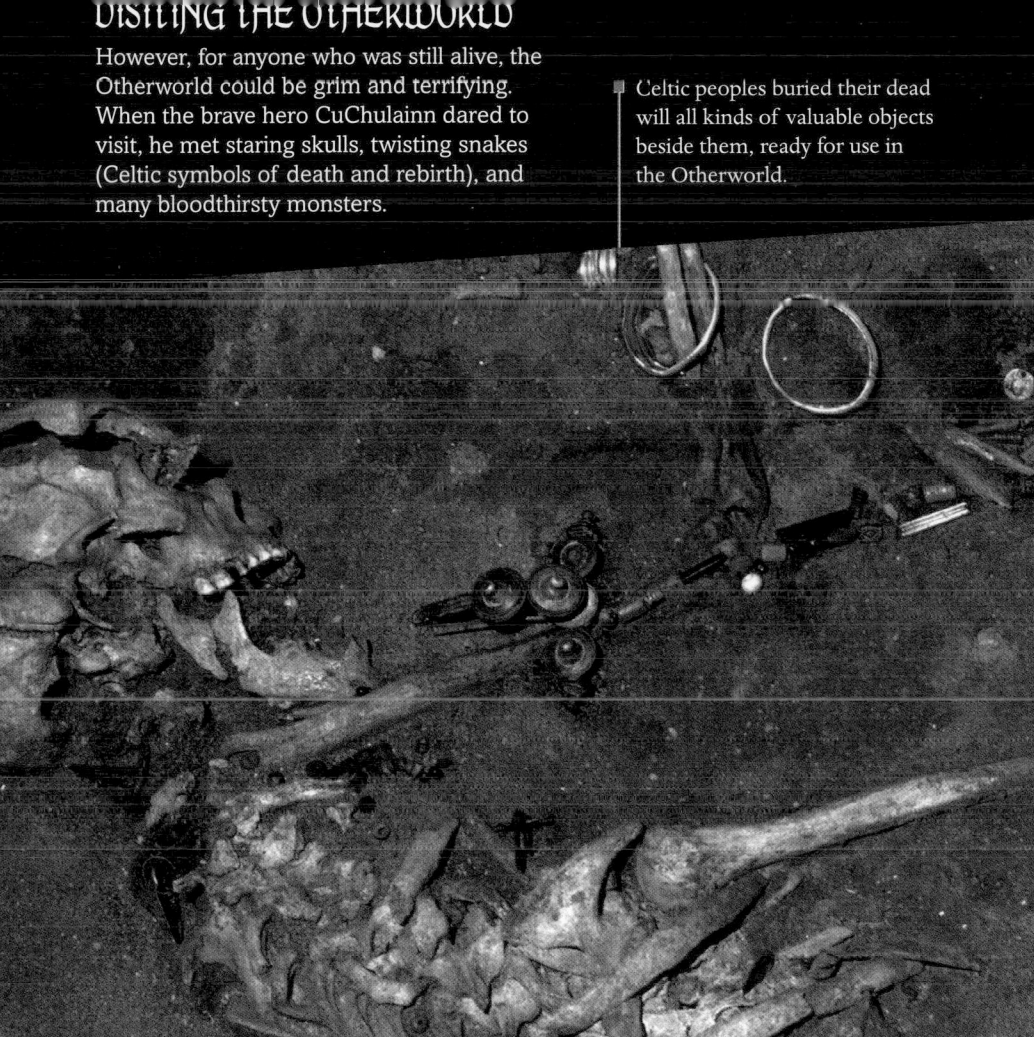

Did you know?

Sprits from the Otherworld warned that death was near. In Scotland and Ireland, they appeared as old women, washing bloody clothes. In Brittany, they took the shape of Korred (little hairy men) and forced living people to dance until they died.

The land of the ever young

It is a lovely morning. A pale sky, and mist on the lake. Calm and still – except for the sound of hoof beats, coming closer, closer.

She rides across the water, beautiful as a dream. A princess, clothed in jewels and shimmering silk. Niamh – Niamh of the Golden Hair.

Warrior Fionn MacCumail is dumbfounded. Then the lady speaks. "Fionn, I want to marry your son. Will he come with me?"

Young Oisin steps forward. He longs for the adventure; he's caught in her spell. They smile, and ride off together – over the lake, across the sea.

Now there's land ahead: a magic garden, an enchanted forest, a castle, rich and tall. There are beautiful people, and a proud king. Food, music, laughter. Night and day, rest and play, they're all together. Sunlight and showers; the rainbow's end.

Niamh speaks again. "Welcome, my dearest. Welcome! Will you make your home with me in the Otherworld, the land of the ever young?"

How can Oisin say no? Here is everything he could ever want – indeed, much, much more. Time passes in bliss, in peace, in pleasure, in dreams.

Is it all utterly perfect? Yes – and no. After a while, Oisin longs to see his father and his friends, just once more. For the first time since they met, Niamh's smile disappears. "Oh my love," she warns. "Yes – yes, go! But never let your feet touch the ground."

Oisin gallops across waves; across dry land. Surely, this is his old house? But it's a ruin, all overgrown! And what is this ancient-looking grave? No! Not his father's? It seems that time passes quickly on earth, much more quickly than in the Otherworld.

As Oisin leans forward in the saddle, he forgets to be careful, and one foot just grazes the ground. In an instant, he is old and grey. One moment more, his bones have turned to dust. He lies beside his father.

CELTIC SURVIVALS

The Celtic way of life flourished in Europe for a thousand years. But by around AD 400, Celtic power disappeared. Celtic tribes were defeated by Roman soldiers, then by peoples living north and east of Celtic lands. At the same time, a new, Christian, religion spread across Europe, bringing new beliefs and powerful, educated priests who strongly disapproved of Celtic ideas. The Celts, now mostly powerless, began to live like their conquerors, sharing their beliefs, and speaking their languages.

Even so, Celtic ideas, designs, words – and myths – did not completely disappear. Celtic kings still ruled Scotland and Ireland until around AD 1000. Craft workers there still used Celtic designs, and Celtic myths and stories were passed down by word of mouth. After around AD 800, they were written down by Christian monks, for anyone to read. This preserved them forever. Celtic languages survived in Scotland, Ireland, Wales, Cornwall, and Brittany. Millions of people living there still speak them today.

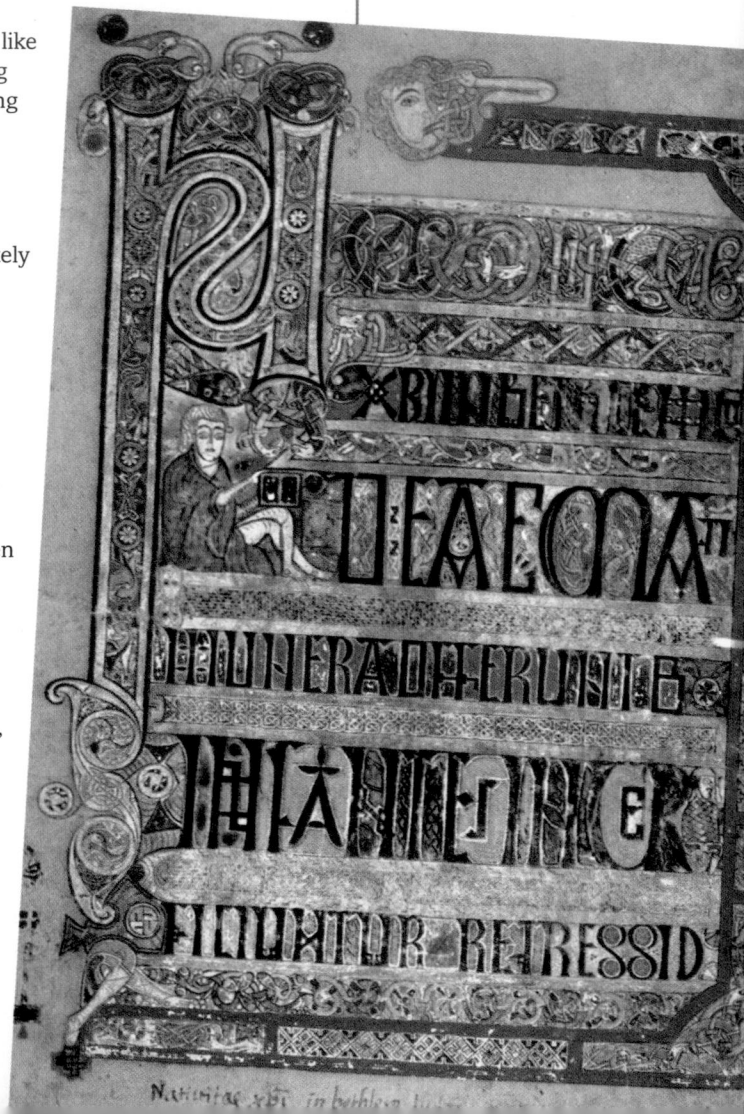

■ This page from a hand-painted manuscript known as the Book of Kells was created by monks who fled from Scotland to Ireland around AD 800. It combines Christian text with ancient Celtic patterns.

MYTH LINKS

Many Celtic myths have survived as fairy tales or the plots of Christmas pantomimes. For example, the well-known story of Jack the Giant Killer was originally a Celtic myth from Cornwall.

This tall stone cross, made in Ireland around AD 920, was carved with Celtic spiral patterns together with pictures of famous characters from Christian Bible stories.

WHO'S WHO?

One of Britain's best-known heroes, King Arthur, may have been based on a Celtic warlord who lived around AD 450. Stories about King Arthur and his knights have been told for over a thousand years. They share many Celtic themes, such as magic weapons, mysterious monsters, shadowy Otherworlds, and warrior pride.

HOW DO WE KNOW?

The Celts did not describe themselves in writing. So how can we find out about them? There are three different kinds of evidence to help us.

We can read eye-witness accounts from ancient Greeks and Romans. We can look at objects made by Celtic craft workers. And we can read Celtic myths that were written down by monks, after the end of Celtic power. But all this evidence has problems. For example, the Greeks and Romans thought the Celts were savage; objects cannot speak; and monks mixed Celtic myths with later Christian ideas.

However, put together, it can still tell us a great deal.

Also, if we read or listen carefully, we can still find clues to tell us about Celtic lives. For example, in one myth, sun-god Lugh demands to enter a Celtic king's fortress. He boasts that he is a carpenter, blacksmith, bodyguard, swordsman, harpist, hero, poet, and historian. That's a very helpful list of all the skills the Celts really valued. It gives us a picture of the ideal Celtic person: clever, brave, artistic, and strong.

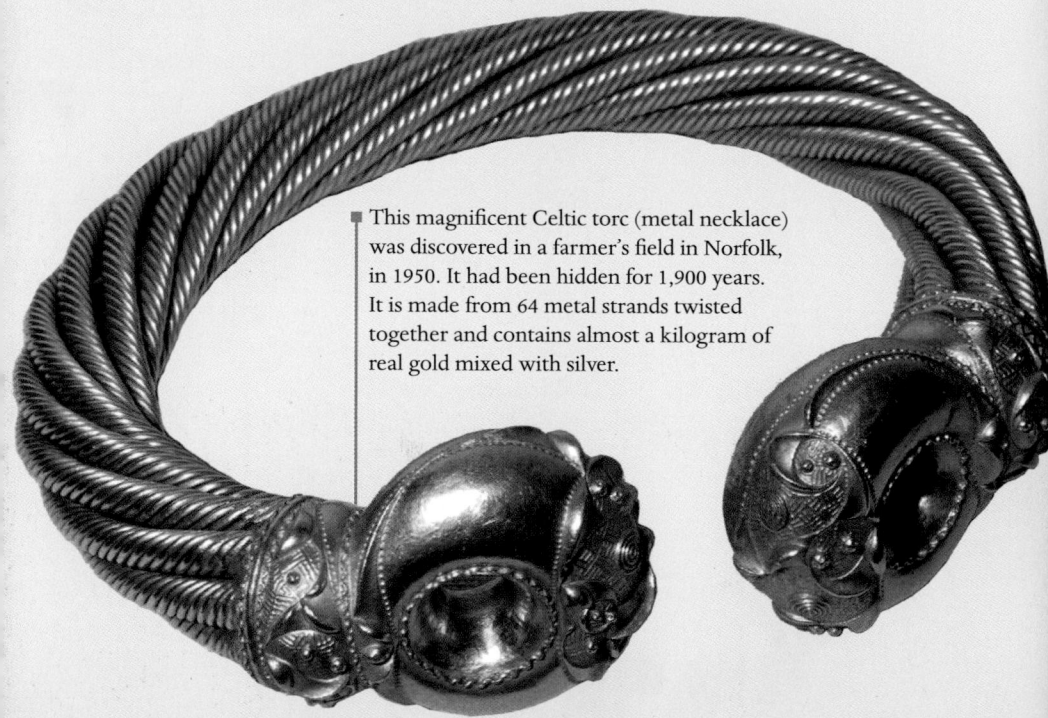

This magnificent Celtic torc (metal necklace) was discovered in a farmer's field in Norfolk, in 1950. It had been hidden for 1,900 years. It is made from 64 metal strands twisted together and contains almost a kilogram of real gold mixed with silver.

Over 1,000 years after the end of Celtic civilization, Celtic myths still feature in films such as the computer-animated *Brave* (released 2012).

Did you know?

Modern English still contains a few Celtic words, such as *gob* (mouth) and *Daddy* (father). And hundreds of names have Celtic origins: Angus, Brian, Bridget, Dylan, Ewan, Gavin, Gwyneth, Jennifer, Kerry, Kevin, Maureen, Morgan, Rhianna, Sweeney, Tristan ... and more!

CHARACTERS AND CREATURES

There are many different ways to pronounce and spell Celtic names. There are Scottish, Irish, and Welsh variations and also ancient and modern versions. Look at the words in brackets for one suggestion of how to say these Celtic names.

GODS, GODDESSES, AND SPIRITS

Cernunnos (*Kur-noo-noss*) Celtic god of wild animals and hunting. He had horns on his head, like a stag.

Dian Cecht (*Dyee-un Kecht*) god of blacksmiths and magic healing

Epona (*Ay-poe-nah*) Celtic goddess who protected horses and their riders. Her name is the origin of the modern word "pony".

Groac'h (*Grah-sh*) evil nature spirit from Brittany, France, who trapped young men in her palace beneath lake waters

Korred Otherworld spirits, described in Breton myths. They forced living people to dance till they died.

Lugh (*Loo*) one of the greatest Celtic gods, clever, wise, and skilled in all the arts and crafts. Often called "shining", like the Sun.

Medb (*Mayve*) Celtic goddess of land, war, and fertility, and a mythical queen. Her name meant "she who intoxicates", and she had many magic powers. She could talk to animals and shape-shift into a male warrior. She could make men weak just by looking at them.

Morrigan (*Mor-ree-gan*) Celtic goddess of love and war. Her name meant "Great Queen". She appeared as a raven, or as an old woman washing bloody clothes. Both were signs of death.

KINGS, QUEENS, AND HEROES

Blodeuwedd (*Blodd-eye-weth*) mythical girl made of flowers; she later became an owl

Boudica (*Boo-dee-kah*) real-life Celtic queen who led warriors to fight Roman invaders of England

Bran (*Brann*) (also known as Bran the Blessed) mythical giant king of Wales. He waded through the sea to Ireland to rescue his sister. After he died in battle, his cut-off, but talking, head guarded his kingdom.

Conchobar Mac Nessa (*Kon-chow-var* or *Connor*) mythical king of Ireland; foster-father of hero CuChulainn. A great warrior and leader of an army. One of the husbands of Queen Medb, but, later, her enemy.

CuChulainn *(Koo-shull-en)* mythical Irish super-hero. An amazing sportsman and fighter. He was doomed to have a short life, full of glory. He fought epic battles against Queen Medb and had many dangerous adventures, including a scary visit to the Otherworld.

Culhwch *(Kull-hoochh)* mythical Welsh prince; he fell in love with a giant's daughter, and had to complete all kinds of dangerous tasks before being allowed to marry her

Fergus *(Fur-guss)* Celtic hero. A giant with a vast appetite. Myths said that, at one meal, he could eat seven cows, seven deer, and seven pigs, and swallow seven cauldrons of drink. His sword was as long as a rainbow.

Fionn Mac Cumail *(Finn Mac Cool)* mythical giant and hero. He led the Fianna (*Fee-yanna*), a band of warriors, on many adventures in Scotland and Ireland. The massive Giant's Causeway rock formation in Northern Ireland is named after him.

Lindow Man name given to a Celtic man who died around 2,250 years ago. His body was found in a bog in northern England.

Nuadu *(Noo-ah-duh)* mythical king in Ireland who lost an arm in battle and replaced it with one made of silver

Vercingetorix *(Vair-sin-geyt-or-ix)* real-life king who led Celtic tribes in France to fight against Roman invaders in 52 BC

DRUIDS

Cathbad *(Kah-bah)* mythical Irish druid. He made prophecies about the future.

Finnegas *(Finn-ay-gus)* mythical druid who educated young hero Fionn. He caught the Salmon of Wisdom.

CREATURE

Tarasque *(Tah–rask)* bloodthirsty, man-eating, mythical monster from Celtic France

GLOSSARY

boar wild pig, usually larger, stronger, and fiercer than pigs on farms

bog area of waterlogged ground. Celtic peoples threw sacrifices – people, animals, prized objects – into bogs.

bronze yellow, shiny metal; an alloy (blend) of copper and tin

bull-sleep Celtic ritual for choosing a king. A man ate bull's flesh and wrapped himself in a bull's hide, then waited for a message in a dream.

carnyx Celtic war trumpet

cauldron huge metal pot, used for cooking or mixing drinks for feasts

champion's portion biggest and best serving of meat at a feast, given to the bravest Celtic warrior

culture way of life shared by a group of people, including language, beliefs, customs, traditions, technology, and artistic designs

doomed fated to have bad luck, or to die

druid powerful, respected Celtic "wise man". Led religious rituals, studied and taught magic and the natural world, and remembered tribal history. Some druids were poets. Some claimed to see into the future.

fertility the power to produce seeds, flowers, babies, and fresh growth of all kinds

goblet large cup used for drinking

hide skin of an animal

High King ruler who was stronger and more powerful than other kings and chieftains, and ruled over them

hurling game similar to hockey, played in Ireland

krater cauldron, used to mix drinks for a feast

massacre brutally kill in large numbers

minstrels professional musicians, singers, and instrumentalists

Otherworld mythical place where Celtic gods and spirits lived, and where the spirits of dead people might go after death

pupil black circle at the centre of each eye

ritual actions done in a special way as part of religious worship or some other important occasion, such as choosing a king

sacrifice something very valuable given to the gods, to ask for their help or to thank them

shape-shift in myths, people or animals changing themselves into different creatures

spring stream of water bubbling up from deep underground

stag male deer; a large, swift, powerful wild animal with huge antlers (bony growths, which look like tree branches) on its head

torc necklace worn by high-ranking Celtic men and women. It was often made of strips of precious metal twisted together.

totem symbol of a tribe, thought to have magic protective powers

tribe group of people who lived as a community and followed a leader. Members of a tribe were sometimes descended from the same ancestor, or believed that they were.

triple counted in threes

FIND OUT MORE

BOOKS

Celtic Tales and Legends, Nicola Baxter and Cathie Shuttleworth (Armadillo, 2012)

The Celtic World (Step Into), Fiona Macdonald, (Southwater, 2009)

Celts (Hands-on History), Joe Fullman (QED, 2010)

The Celts (The History Detective Investigates), Philip Steele (Wayland, 2011)

Favourite Irish Legends for Children, Yvonne Carroll, Fiona Waters, and Felicity Trotman (Gill & Macmillan, 2010)

WEBSITES

www.asterix.com
Asterix, the Gaulish (French Celtic) cartoon character created in 1959, has featured in over 30 books, and has his own website.

www.bbc.co.uk/history/interactive/animations/wetwang_chariot/index.shtml
This site tells how a Celtic war-chariot was excavated.

www.bbc.co.uk/learningzone/clips/life-in-pre-roman-britain/3679.html
This video shows what Celtic houses and farms were like.

www.bbc.co.uk/wales/celts/index.shtml?1
Games, animations, and information about the Celts who lived in Wales.

celts.mrdonn.org/dailylife.html
This website provides a good introduction to Celtic culture.

PLACES TO VISIT

The British Museum
Great Russell Street
London WC1B 3DG
Visit the Iron Age galleries at the British Museum to see objects made by Celtic craft workers.

Butser Ancient Farm
Chalton Lane
Chalton
Hampshire PO8 0BG
Visit this replica Iron-Age farm to see what farmers' lives were like in about 300 BC.

The National Museum of Scotland
Chambers Street
Edinburgh EH1 1JF
This museum has information on Celtic culture in Scotland.

The National Museum of Wales
Cathays Park
Cardiff CF10 3NP
This museum's Iron Age collection focuses on Celtic culture in Wales.

FURTHER RESEARCH

Which Celtic myth did you like reading most in this book? Which characters did you find most interesting? Can you find out about any more myths in which these characters appear? You could look in the books or on the websites listed here, or even visit some of the places mentioned. You could also try retelling your favourite myth in a new way, such as a diary, a cartoon strip, or a newspaper report.

INDEX